Busy Machines

Written by Amy Johnson

MILES KELLY

First published in 2019 by Miles Kelly Publishing Ltd
Harding's Barn, Bardfield End Green, Thaxted, Essex, CM6 3PX, UK

Thsi edition printed 2021

4 6 8 10 9 7 5 3

Publishing Director Belinda Gallagher
Creative Director Jo Cowan
Editorial Director Rosie Neave
Senior Editor Amy Johnson
Senior Designer Rob Hale
Image Manager Liberty Newton
Production Jennifer Brunwin
Reprographics Stephan Davis
Assets Lorraine King

ISBN 978-1-78617-897-8

Printed in China

British Library Cataloguing-in-Publication Data
A catalogue record for this book is available from the British Library

ACKNOWLEDGEMENTS
The publishers would like to thank the following artists
who have contributed to this book:
Diggers: Kirsten Collier
Rescue: Steven Wood (Advocate Art)
Tractors: Ela Smietanka (Advocate Art)
Trucks: Craig Shuttlewood (The Bright Agency)

Made with paper from a sustainable forest

www.mileskelly.net

Diggers

Squelch, scoop and rumble along with diggers, dumpers, loaders and lifters.

Ready to build!

All day long, machines are hard at work on the building site. There are diggers and dumpers, loaders and lifters.

They SCRAPE...

Excavator

Crane

Concrete mixer

Dumper truck

and RATTLE...

and RUMBLE.

Bulldozer

5

Diggers at work

Most **excavators** have caterpillar tracks that keep them steady on bumpy ground.

Backhoe

A **backhoe loader** has an arm for digging at the back and a bucket for scooping at the front.

Tractor

Loader bucket

This is an **underwater excavator**. It sits on special floats and scoops sand and mud from swamps and shallow rivers.

SQUELCH!

Float

Wheeled excavators can work on hard ground that heavy caterpillar tracks would destroy.

I lift my cab to give the driver a better view.

7

Monster miner

This is one of the world's biggest machines! It's called a **bucket wheel excavator**. It is used in mines to dig out huge amounts of soil and rock.

Conveyor belts carry the rock away

The bucket wheel is attached to a long arm

The heavy excavator sits on lots of caterpillar tracks that crawl along

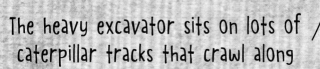

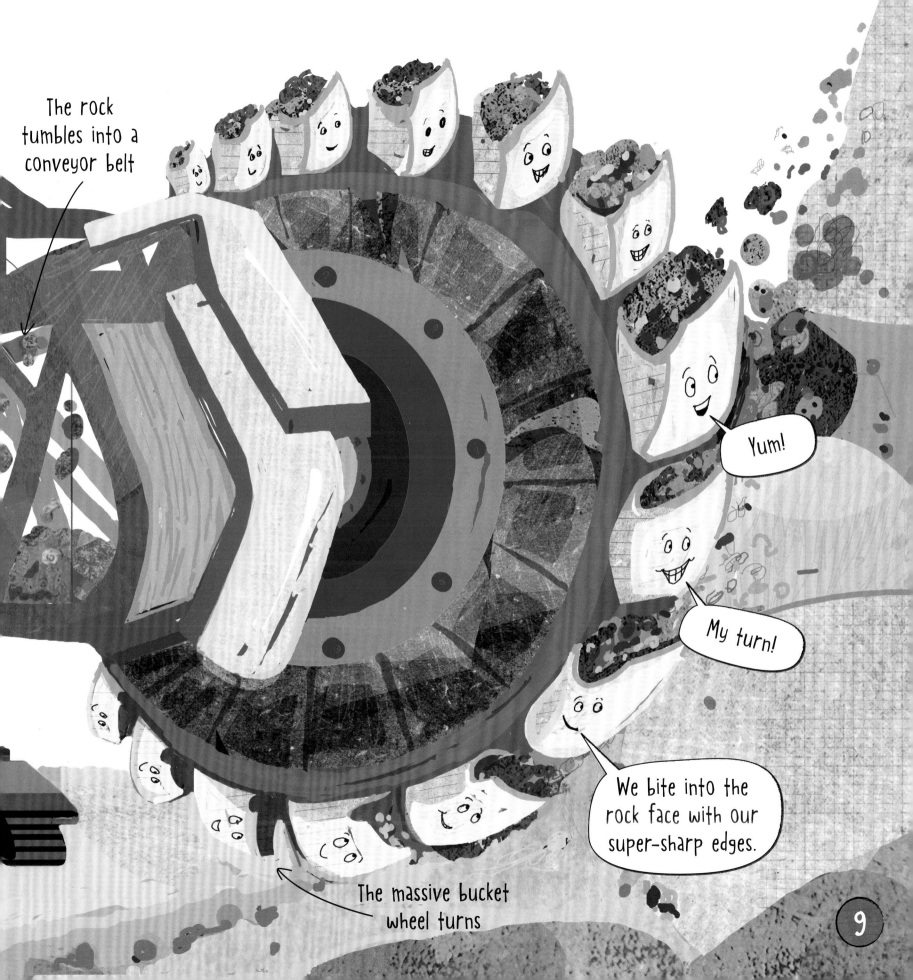

Keep it moving

Meet the tough transporters – machines made for lifting, moving, shifting and scooping.

Forklift

Backhoe loader

Wheel loader

Giant bulldozer

Boom lift

Bulldozer

Dumper truck

Skid-steer loader

Log loader

Earth scraper

Tracked loader

All about excavators

Munching up the ground, digging holes and scooping up heavy loads, **excavators** are very busy building machines.

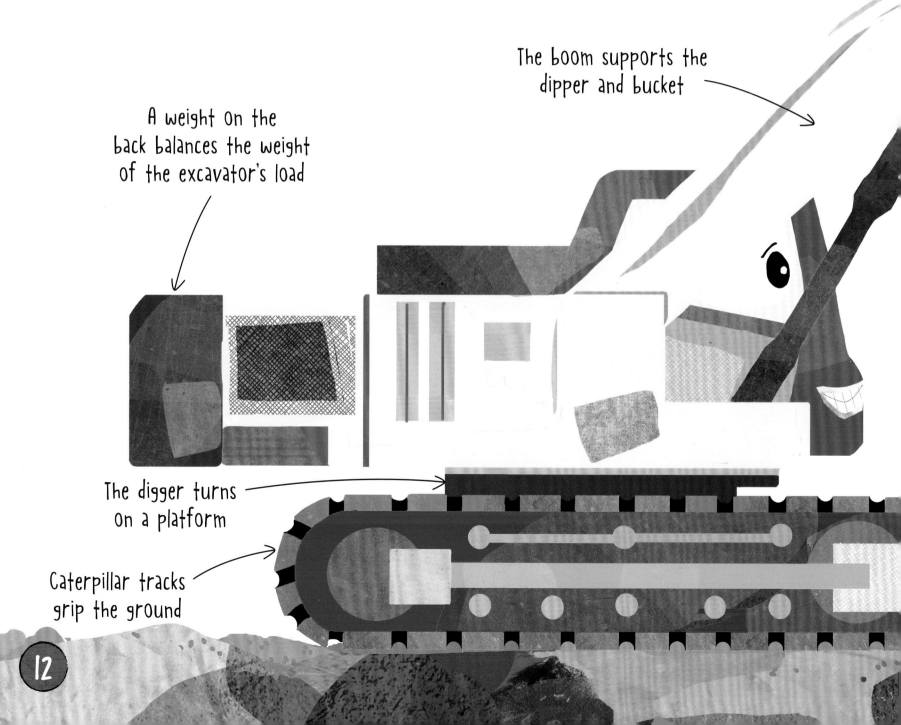

The boom supports the dipper and bucket

A weight on the back balances the weight of the excavator's load

The digger turns on a platform

Caterpillar tracks grip the ground

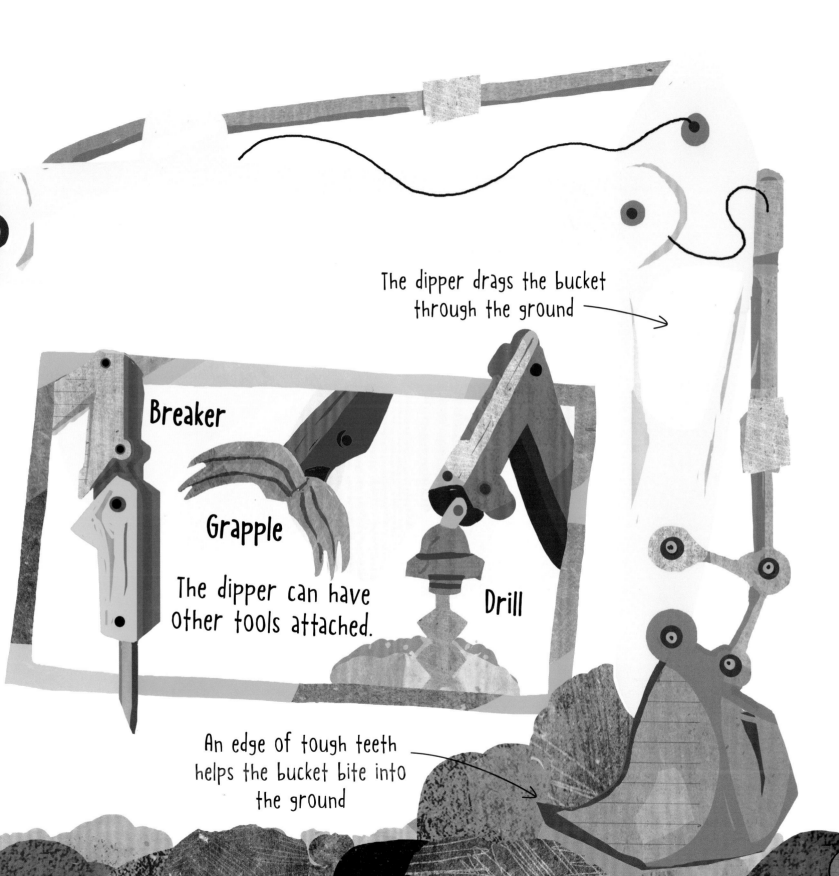

The dipper drags the bucket through the ground

Breaker

Grapple

The dipper can have other tools attached.

Drill

An edge of tough teeth helps the bucket bite into the ground

13

Busy machines!

Find your favourite building machine!

15

Rock busters

Deep in a massive pit, it's the job of tough machines to dig rock from the ground.

Massive **dumper trucks** carry away huge amounts of rock.

A rock crusher breaks up big pieces of rock and shoots out smaller bits.

Using a big metal blade, **bulldozers** push earth and rock out of the way.

Excavators scoop out rock and load it into the dumper trucks.

Wheel loaders move rocks to the dumper trucks or the crusher.

Grapples are used to pick up big rocks.

17

sky high

Tower cranes stay in one spot for months at a time, working high above the ground. They help build very tall buildings.

These blocks balance the weight

The operator has to climb a ladder all the way up to the cab

This tall tower is called a mast

The arm is called a jib. It moves up and down and from side to side

The main arm is called a boom

All about dumper trucks

One of the biggest building machines, dumper trucks are always on the go. They carry great piles of earth, rubble and rock.

The box tilts up to let its load slide out.

Huge tyres give plenty of grip

The canopy protects the cab and engine from falling rocks

Powerful engine

There are ladders for the driver to reach the cab

21

on the road

A new road is taking shape. Massive earth-movers have cleared the way – now it's time to start building!

1 Dirt is added. Bulldozers move and shape the earth.

2 The grader uses its long blade to make a flat surface.

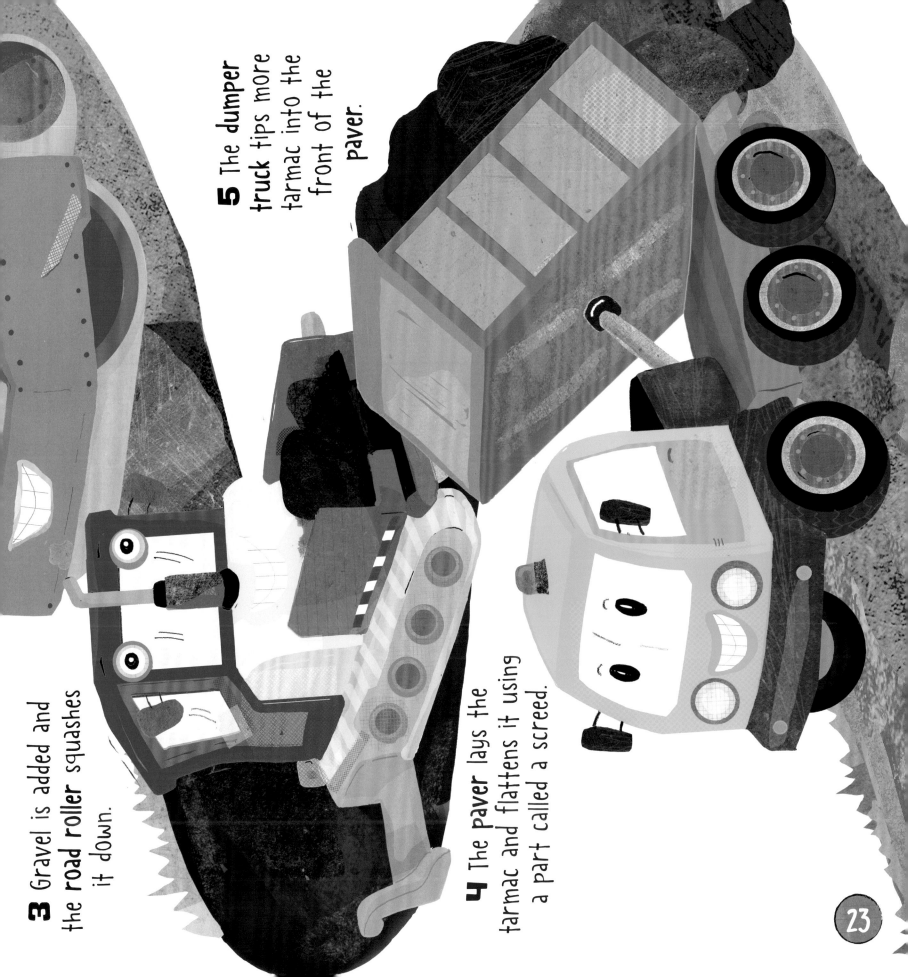

3 Gravel is added and the **road roller** squashes it down.

4 The **paver** lays the tarmac and flattens it using a part called a screed.

5 The dumper truck tips more tarmac into the front of the paver.

smash, crash, crumble

It takes a crew of demolition excavators to tear old buildings down! They have extra-long arms for reaching up high.

First, **skid-steer loaders** take apart the insides of a building.

Then the **excavators** get to work!

Excavators use different tools for different jobs. I'm a pulverizer. I'm great at chomping through concrete and metal!

Walking wonder

To a **walking excavator**, no terrain is too tough! It tackles water, unsteady ground and steep slopes.

On the end of the boom is a bucket or another tool for digging

The boom can also work as an extra leg, stretching across big gaps

Having four legs means I can dig in places other machines can't reach!

Rescue

Sound the sirens and join the machines on their daring rescue missions.

To the rescue!

If there's an emergency, there are many kinds of vehicles that may come to help!

Engines ROAR...

Fire engine

police patrol

On the go and on the look-out, these vehicles help the police do their jobs.

Dog unit car

<<<<DOG PATROL>>>>

Mobile command centre

Motorbike

Traffic car

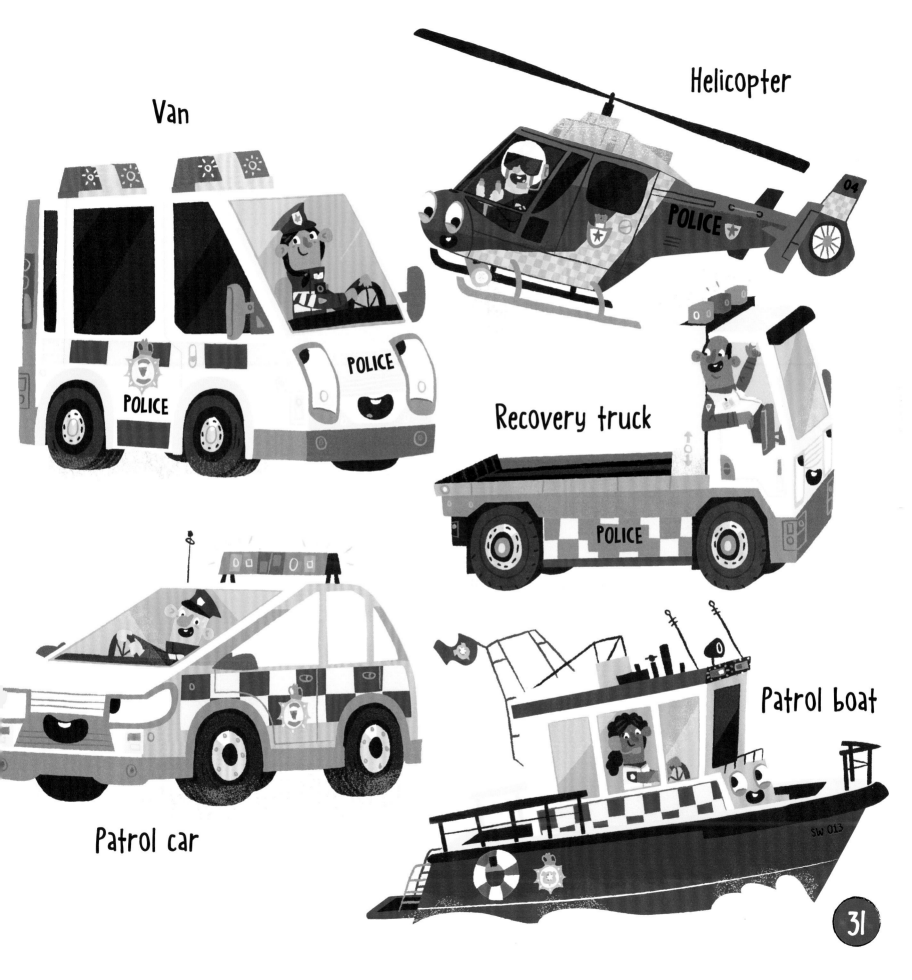

Van

Helicopter

Recovery truck

Patrol car

Patrol boat

31

All about lifeboats

When people get into trouble on the water, a lifeboat will head out to help them.

The aerial picks up signals so the crew can talk to the lifeboat station and other boats

Offshore lifeboats are used at sea. They're built to be speedy and to handle strong winds and waves

Y-166

RNLI-11

Big lifeboats carry a smaller one for rescues in shallow water

The lifeboat can quickly right itself if it capsizes! It has special water tanks that weigh the bottom of the boat down.

The boat sits low in the water so people can be easily reached

RNLI-11

The hull (body) of the boat is very strong

SPLASH!

01

Ambulance in action

If someone is sick or injured, an **ambulance** must be able to reach them in super-quick time.

Rapid response car

I carry machines and medicine to look after the patient until the ambulance arrives.

A **rapid response car** can often get to an emergency even more quickly than an ambulance.

34

Speedy **paramedic motorcycles** can nip through traffic or along narrow roads. They are often first on the scene.

Paramedic motorcycle

074

Ambulance

Once the **ambulance** arrives, the paramedics get ready to move the patient onboard.

35

Airport emergency

Planes carry tonnes of fuel, so a fire onboard is especially dangerous. Airport fire trucks can race to the rescue in minutes. They carry crew, equipment and huge amounts of water and foam.

4

Water and foam are stored in here

Hoses used by firefighters are in here

Nozzles under the truck can put out fire on the ground

The cabin can fit five crew members

This sharp nozzle can punch through the wall of a plane. It is attached to an extra-long arm

WHOOSH!

Nozzles spray foam to smother the fire

The heavy truck has six wheels

37

Busy machines!

Pick your favourite rescue vehicle!

FIRE

2

DOG PATROL

POLICE

RNLI-11

4

39

Mountain rescue

Some climbers are lost in the mountains! A search and rescue crew gets to work to track them down.

Offroad trucks can take on steep, slippery ground. They carry stretchers and first aid kits.

A **minibus** carries rescuers and equipment.

Blades whirring, the **helicopter** searches from above. Suddenly, it gets the call — the climbers have been spotted!

I hover in the air and lift people to safety using a winch.

AMBULANCE

Quad bikes can speed over all kinds of tricky ground.

All about ambulances

It's the job of an **ambulance** to get sick or injured people to hospital as fast as possible.

Sirens and flashing lights warn other vehicles to give way

The crew use a radio to talk to the control centre or hospital

Ambulances have bright markings or symbols so they can be easily seen

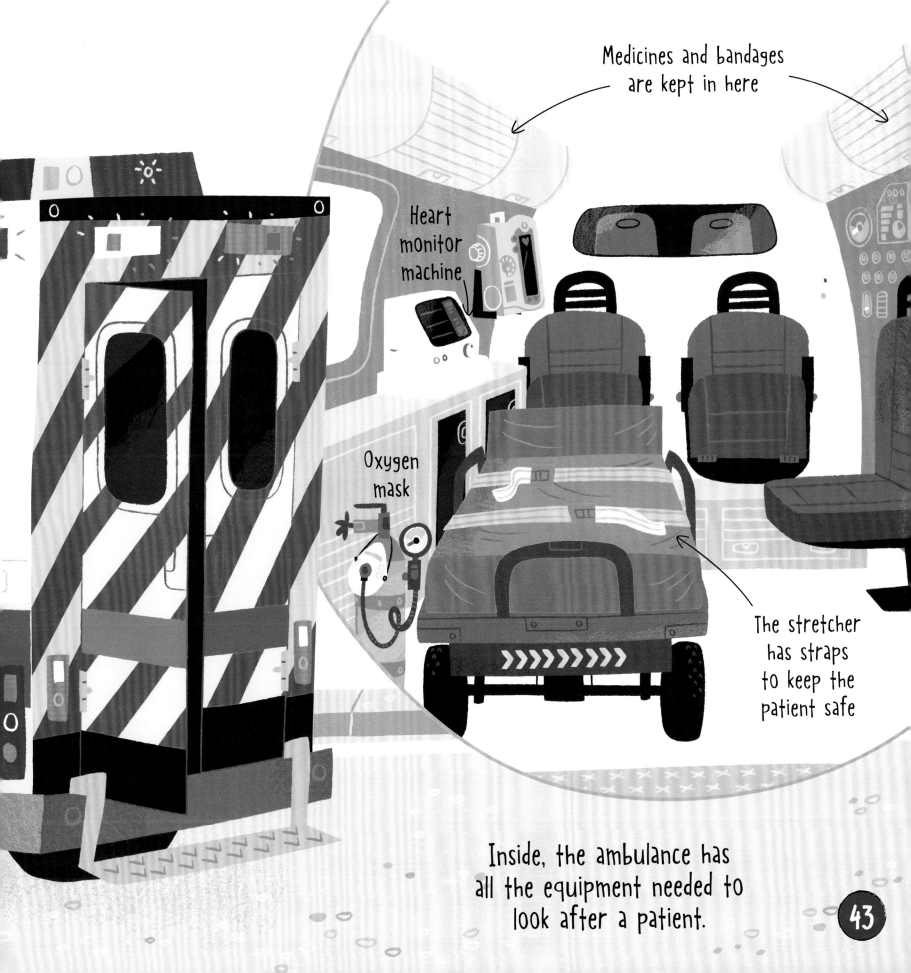

Medicines and bandages
are kept in here

Heart
monitor
machine

Oxygen
mask

The stretcher
has straps
to keep the
patient safe

Inside, the ambulance has
all the equipment needed to
look after a patient.

43

On the water

Climb aboard! On rivers, at the coast and further out to sea, there are rescue vessels ready to help.

Offshore lifeboat

RNLI-11

Inshore lifeboat

B-756

Rescue hovercraft

Lifeguard rescue boat

44

Fireboat

FIRE

2

Police patrol boat

I create a cushion of air that holds me above the waves.

-01-

Ship's lifeboat

Ship's life raft

Coastguard patrol boat

COASTGUARD

45

Fighting fire

A fire is blazing, flames crackle and spark, but the fire engines are on the scene!

Firefighters work from the platform

Ladder trucks have an extra-long ladder that slides up to tackle flames in tall buildings.

Legs to keep the truck steady

Hose

Fire engines carry equipment and some water to tackle the blaze. They get more water from fire hydrants connected to underground pipes.

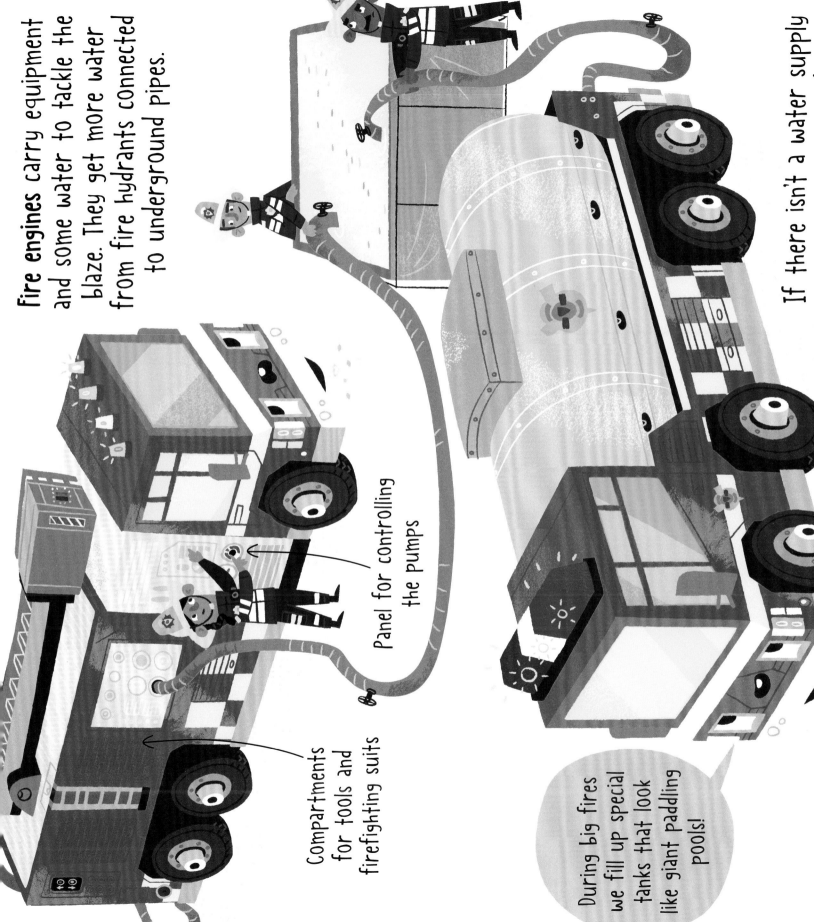

Panel for controlling the pumps

Compartments for tools and firefighting suits

During big fires we fill up special tanks that look like giant paddling pools!

If there isn't a water supply nearby, **water tankers** are used. They carry huge amounts of water to the scene.

47

Rescue flight

An air ambulance helicopter can reach sick or injured people and get them quickly to hospital.

Firefighting planes drop water and special chemicals ahead of forest fires to stop them spreading.

Search and rescue helicopters find people in trouble and make daring rescues.

Police helicopters help track down suspects, search for missing people, and keep an eye on big crowds.

It's easy for me to keep up with a speedy suspect!

49

Snow searcher

Tough **all-terrain vehicles** are often used to rescue people stranded in heavy snow.

There is room inside for 17 people

I'm great at snowy search and rescue as I don't get stuck.

Two sections joined together move over drifts and slopes more easily

Wide, tough tracks stop the vehicle sinking

Tractors

Trundle through the fields with tremendous tractors and farm machines.

Tractor power!

On the farm, tractors work busily with other machines to get jobs done.

Front loader

They TRUNDLE...

Baler

Hedge trimmer

and JUDDER...

and CHUG.

Tractor

Trailer

53

All about tractors

Tractors are very powerful! They are mainly used to pull other farm machines.

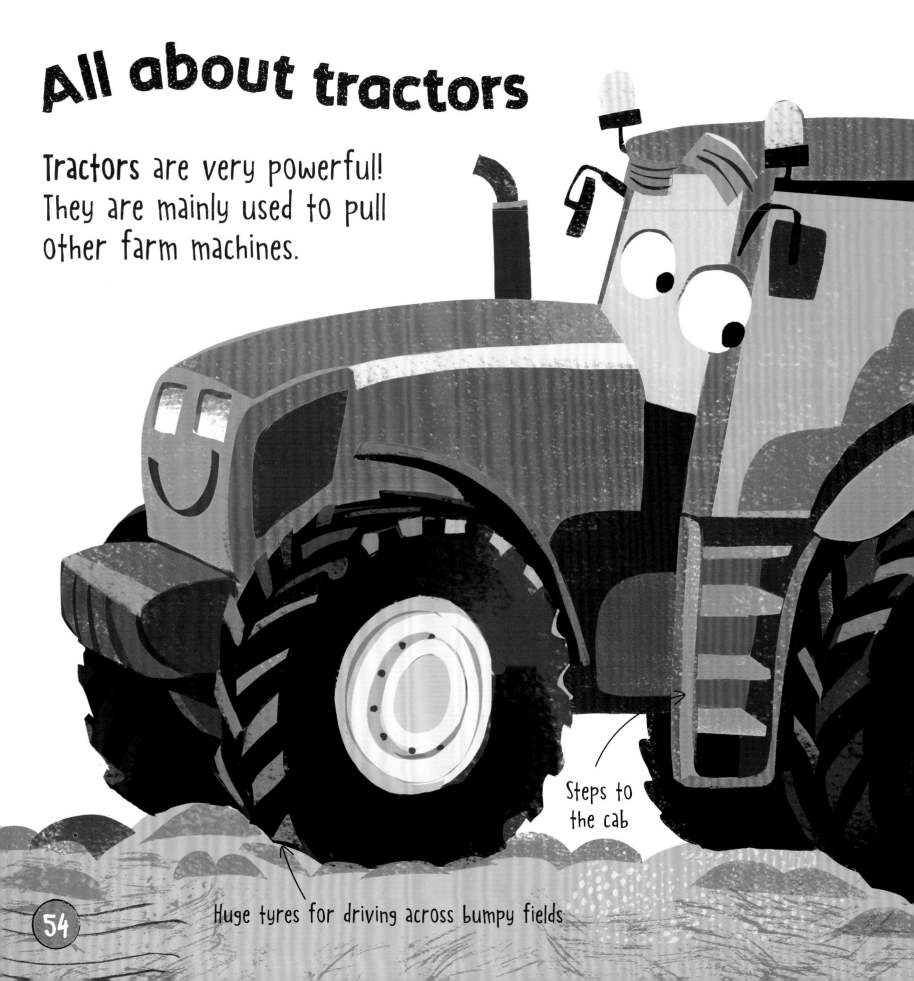

Steps to the cab

Huge tyres for driving across bumpy fields

The cab is high up so the driver can see all around

Mudguards stop earth flying everywhere

Different machines are joined to the back of the tractor.

Balers make hay, straw or grass into bales

Seed drills plant seeds

Ploughs turn the soil

The plough makes rows called furrows as it is pulled through the soil

55

Riding high

Tall crops need tall tractors! This **crop sprayer** has extra-big wheels so it can travel above plants like sunflowers.

Nozzles on the boom spray the crops to protect them from disease and help them grow

The sprayer's arm is called a boom

Earth work

Before seeds are planted, these machines help to prepare the soil.

Ploughs break up and turn the earth.

A stone picker removes stones from the soil.

sowing seeds

The fields have been ploughed — now they're ready for planting.

Seed drills drop seeds into the ground in rows then cover them with soil.

60

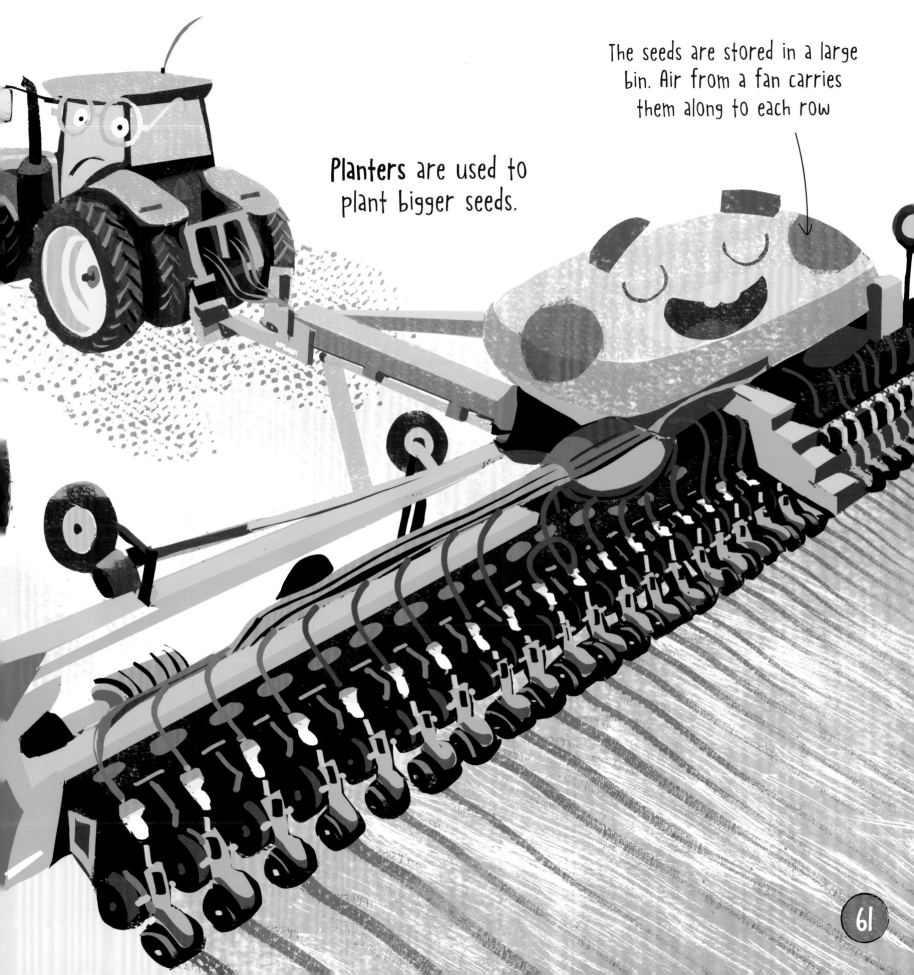

Planters are used to plant bigger seeds.

The seeds are stored in a large bin. Air from a fan carries them along to each row

Busy machines!

find your favourite farm machine!

63

Super tractors!

Big Bud is the largest farm tractor in the world. It was built in the USA over 40 years ago. It has a super-powerful engine and huge tyres.

Tracked tractors have tough rubber tracks that don't squash the ground as much as wheels.

Harvesters are used in forests to fell trees. They have a long arm that bends and a claw-like grabbing tool.

65

Harvest time

Combine harvesters cut crops such as wheat and oats, and then separate the grains from the stalks.

Potatoes bounce along a conveyor belt on the **potato harvester**, out into a trailer.

Chute unloads into a trailer

Grass is blown into a chute

Forage harvesters are used to gather grass and corn for animal feed.

Cotton bale

Cotton harvesters pick fluffy white clumps of cotton from their plants.

All about balers

When a field is full of hay bales, it means a **baler** has been hard at work.

The baler is pulled by the tractor

2 Inside, the hay is squashed and bundled into shape by rollers

1 The baler picks up hay as it moves over it

Bales are collected by special **bale-handler tractors.** Some can lift six in One go!

3 The back opens and the finished bale rolls out

Lots of jobs

It takes many kinds of machines to keep a busy farm running.

I'm great for clearing straw, mud and muck!

Skid-steer loader

Trailer

Orchard tractor

Muck spreader

The boom slides out to reach high-up things

Boom lift

Pick-up truck

Utility tractor

Rotary mower

71

Combine team

When grain is ripe, it takes whole teams of combines to harvest big areas.

The crops need to be harvested quickly so less is wasted

Trucks

Take to the road to meet tough travellers and mega movers.

Out and about

The roads are busy with travelling trucks, big and small, carrying all kinds of loads.

Flatbed truck

They THUNDER...

Pick-up truck

and TRUNDLE...

Van

Lorry

and GROWL!

Dumper truck

75

Tremendous transporters

Rumbling along, these tough trucks haul heavy cargo.

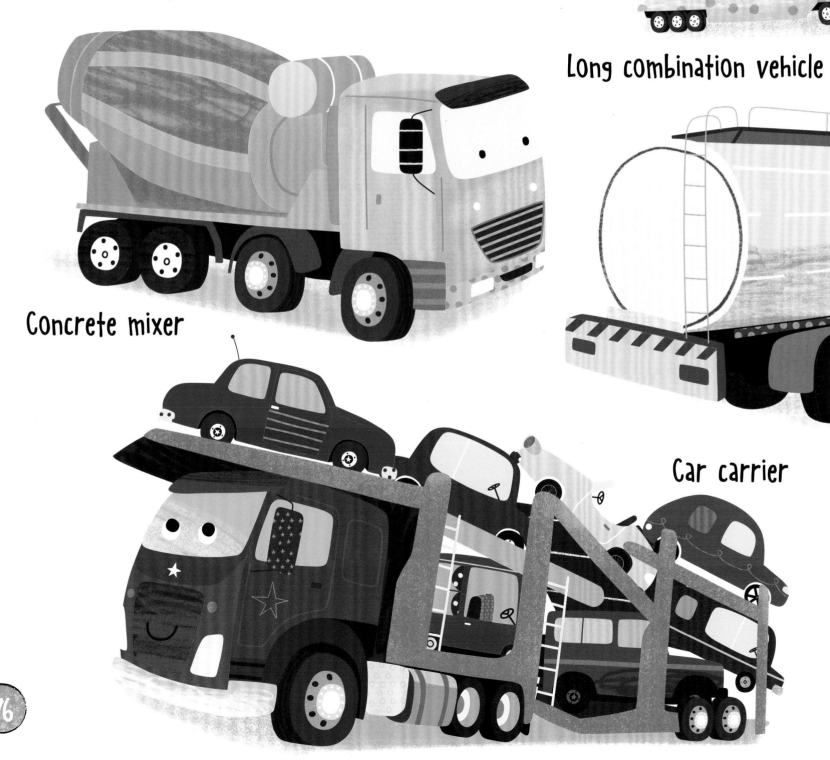

Long combination vehicle

Concrete mixer

Car carrier

Container truck

Fuel tanker

Low loader

Clearing the streets

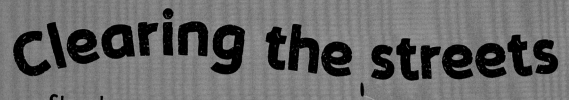

Street sweepers have speedy spinning brushes that scrub away dirt and rubbish.

Spinning brush ➔

WHOOSH!

When heavy snow hits, **snow ploughs** work to clear the way.

In cold weather, gritting lorries spread salt on the roads to stop them icing over.

Recycling trucks collect the things you put in your recycling bin.

Monster mayhem

Brightly painted trucks jump and spin, landing on giant tyres – welcome to the **monster truck** show!

In races, two trucks take on tracks with sharp bends and big jumps

Shock absorbers keep the truck body steady

The trucks do stunts like wheelies and backflips

The body is a big car
or pick-up truck

Massive
off-road tyres

81

All about lorries

Lorries are big vehicles that carry cargo over long distances. There's lots to be done before the lorry sets out.

This lorry has soft sides that can be opened like a curtain

A forklift truck loads the cargo

Cargo is kept inside the trailer

The trailer is attached to a tractor unit

The driver sits in the cab

There is space inside the cab for drivers to rest and eat — they need to take breaks so they don't get too tired.

Powerful engine

Busy machines!

85

Delivery time

These hard-working trucks are always on the go. They have plenty of deliveries to make!

The **post van** has lots of parcels and letters to be delivered.

Cargo area works like a giant fridge

Refrigerated trucks keep things cold, so they transport food and drink such as fruit and milk.

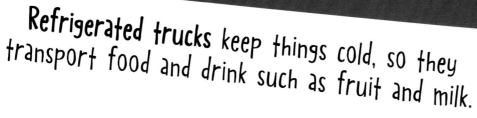

A **removal van** can be stacked high with furniture.

Delivery trucks deliver parcels that people have ordered online.

Milk floats aren't used as much today, but you might have seen one!

Massive movers

High up in the mountains in Chile, two amazing trucks do a special job — they transport huge telescope antennas.

Each antenna weighs 100 tonnes! Moving it takes very powerful engines

Each transporter truck is 20 metres long — that's about the length of five small cars

This transporter is called Lore. Its twin is named Otto

Lore

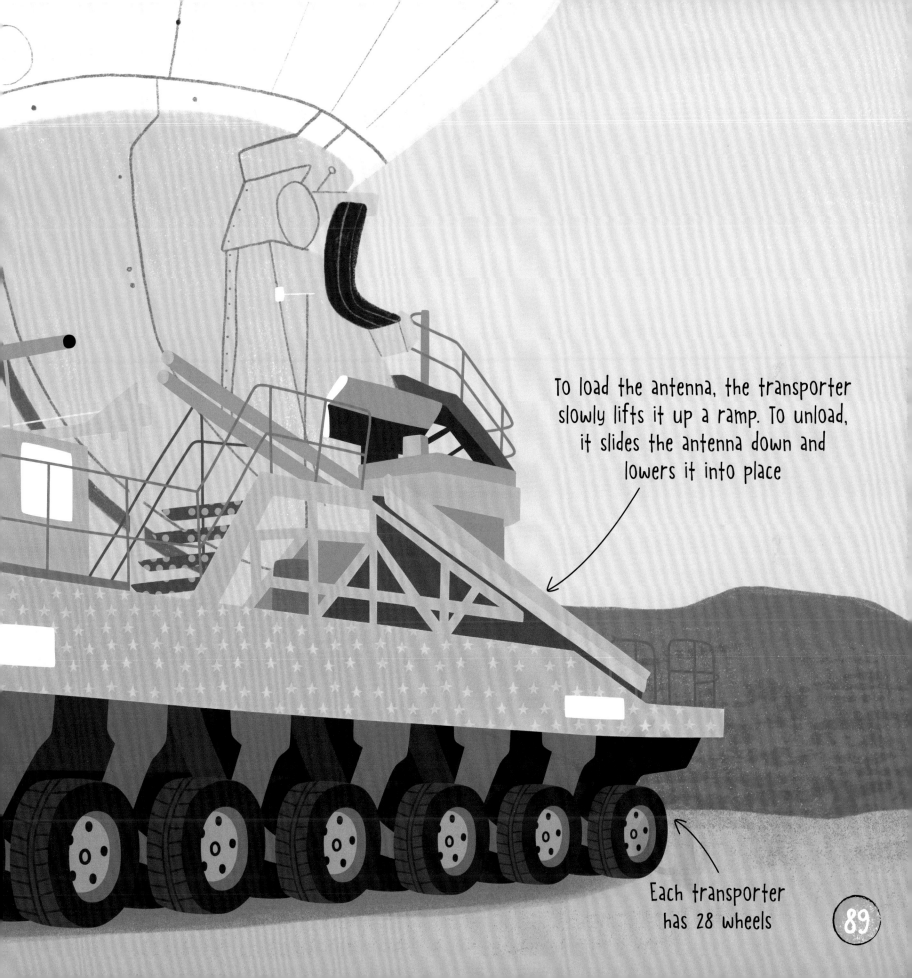

To load the antenna, the transporter slowly lifts it up a ramp. To unload, it slides the antenna down and lowers it into place

Each transporter has 28 wheels

Hard at work

Some trucks are built to take on the toughest jobs, from hauling rocks to fighting fires.

All-terrain truck

Logging truck

Military truck

Fire engine

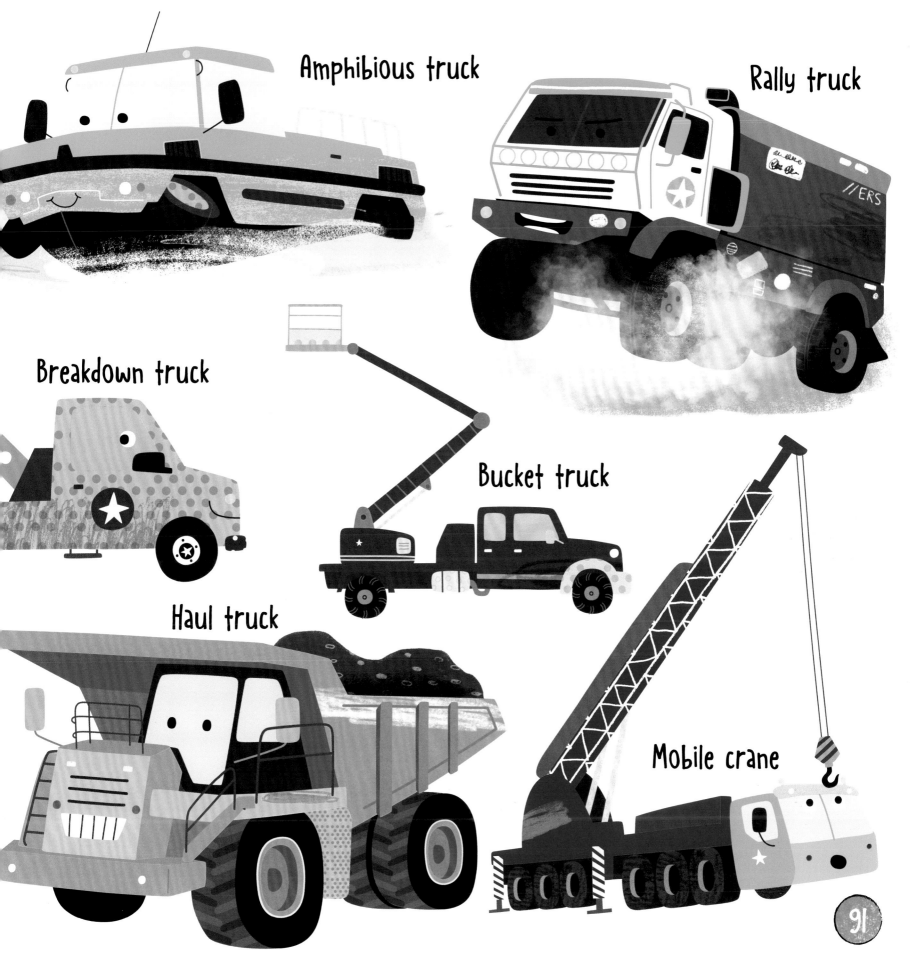

Amphibious truck

Rally truck

Breakdown truck

Bucket truck

Haul truck

Mobile crane

All about car carriers

With shiny new cars packed onto its decks, the towering **car carrier** is ready to go!

Some car carriers have room for 12 cars at once!

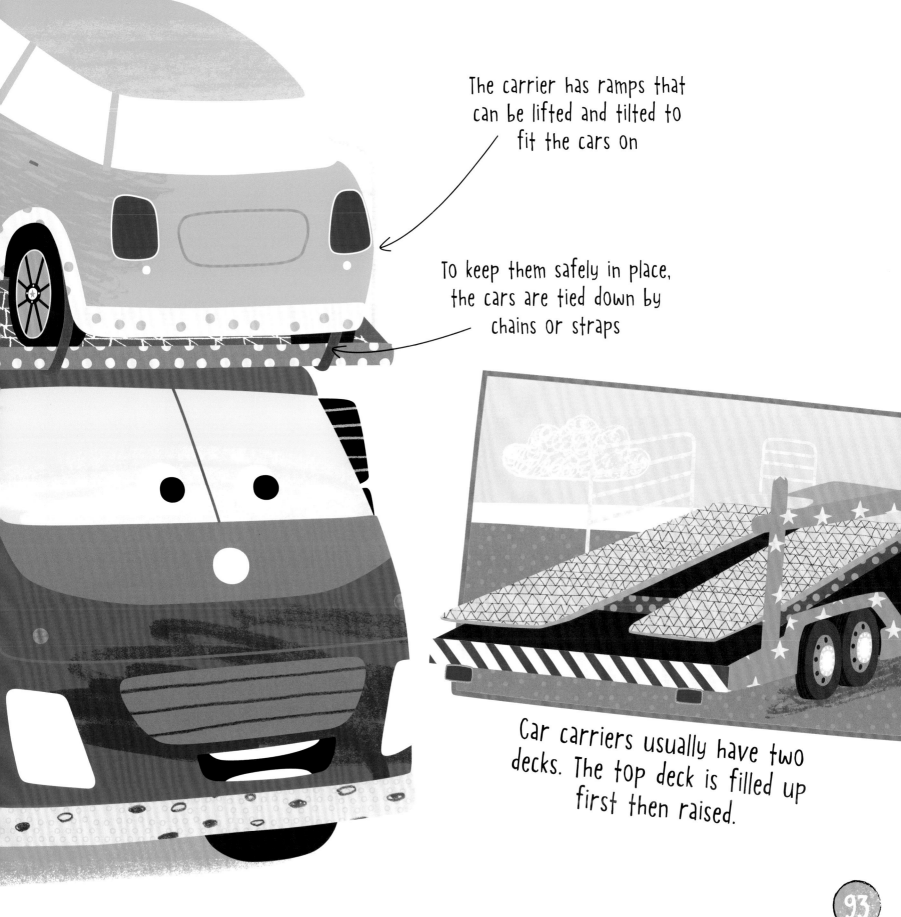

The carrier has ramps that can be lifted and tilted to fit the cars on

To keep them safely in place, the cars are tied down by chains or straps

Car carriers usually have two decks. The top deck is filled up first then raised.

Turnaround trucks

A plane has just landed – no time to lose! A team of hard-working trucks get it ready for the next flight.

A **de-icing truck** sprays a special mixture to melt any ice. Its arm can reach the top of the plane.

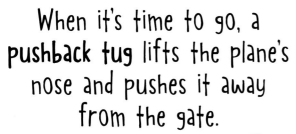

When it's time to go, a **pushback tug** lifts the plane's nose and pushes it away from the gate.

Mobile stairs are driven to the plane for the passengers to board.

Fuel is pumped into the plane by a **refueler**.

Luggage is driven to the plane on a **baggage truck**. It then goes up to the cargo hold on a **belt loader**.

Truck race!

It's time for the trucks to take to the track! They battle it out to be first to the finish.

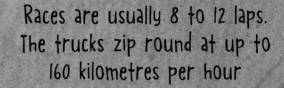

We speed around the circuit, weaving past each other.

Races are usually 8 to 12 laps. The trucks zip round at up to 160 kilometres per hour